Residential Care Homes

Health and Safety Series booklet HS(G) 104

HSE BOOKS

© *Crown copyright 1993*

Applications for reproduction should be made in writing to:

Copyright Unit, Her Majesty's Stationery Office,
St Clements House, 2-16 Colegate, Norwich NR3 1BQ

First published 1993
Reprinted 1994, 1995, 1998, 1999

ISBN 0 7176 0673 2

This guidance is issued by the Health and Safety Executive. Following the guidance is not compulsory and you are free to take other action. But if you do follow the guidance you will normally be doing enough to comply with the law. Health and safety inspectors seek to secure compliance with the law and may refer to this guidance as illlustrating good practice.

Contents

Introduction ... 1

Legal duties ... 3

Duties of employers to employees ... 4

Consultation with employees ... 4

Health and safety records and documentation ... 4

Duties of employers to people not in
their employment ... 5

Duties of self-employed people ... 5

Duties of people in charge of premises ... 5

Duties of employees ... 5

Contractors ... 6

Health, safety and welfare of residents ... 7

Management of health and safety ... 9

Staff training ... 11

Incidents ... 13

Notification of injuries and dangerous
occurrences ... 14

Specified injuries ... 14

Dangerous occurrences ... 15

Notification of reportable diseases ... 15

Reporting in writing ... 16

Record keeping ... 16

RIDDOR and non-RIDDOR accidents ... 16

Notification of accidents to Registration and
Inspection Unit ... 18

Occupational health ... 19

First aid ... 20

Control of Substances Hazardous to Health
Regulations (COSHH) 1988 ... 20

COSHH assessment ... 21

Clinical waste ... 22

Blood-borne infections ... 24

Drugs and medicines ... 25

Asbestos ... 25

Water temperatures ... 27

Legionnaires' disease ... 28

Scalding ... 28

Acceptable risk ... 29

Surface temperatures ... 29

Manual handling ... 30

Avoidance of manual handling ... 31

Making an assessment ... 32

Reducing the risk of injury ... 32

The task ... 32

The load ... 33

The working environment ... 33

Individual capabilities ... 34

General working environment ... 35

Floors ... 36

Stairs ... 36

Lighting ... 37

Ventilation ... 37

Temperature ... 37

Windows ... 38

Doors ... 38

Lifts ... 38

Stairlifts ... 39

Accommodation for clothing ... 40

Staff rest rooms ... 40

Smoking in the home ... 40

Sanitary conveniences and washing facilities ... 41

Radon gas ... 41

Central heating systems ... 43

Gas safety ... 44

Liquid petroleum gas (LPG) ... 44

Electrical safety ... 45

Fixed electrical installations ... 45

Portable equipment ... 46

Kitchen safety ... 48

Layout ... 49

Floors ... 49

Equipment ... 49

Use of pesticides in kitchens ... 50

Laundry safety ... 51

Machinery ... 52

Handling soiled laundry ... 52

Outdoor health and safety ... 53

Violence to staff ... 56

Appendix 1

Guidance on safety policy statements ... 59

Appendix 2

Training check list ... 60

Appendix 3

Your questions answered ... 61

Appendix 4

Self audit check list ... 63

Appendix 5

Example form F2508 for reporting injuries and

dangerous occurrences ... 67

Appendix 6

Example form F2508A for reporting

cases of disease ... 69

Appendix 7

Factors/questions when making an

assessment of manual handling operations ... 71

Appendix 8

References ... 73

Introduction

1   This booklet is intended for both owners and managers of residential care homes and for employees and safety representatives. It should help them to understand and meet their duties under health and safety legislation. It describes the main risks associated with machinery, equipment, substances and work practices which are found in residential care homes and what should be done to safeguard both workers and residents. It has been produced by the Health and Safety Executive Local Authority Unit after wide consultation with local authority registration and inspection officers, employers, trade unions and other interested organisations.

2   The residential care sector caters for a wide range of needs and in developing this guidance it has been necessary to concentrate on those establishments in the local authority, private and voluntary sector. The booklet is not aimed at nursing homes although many of the activities described in the guidance may occur in these homes. It is hoped that a single document covering those health and safety issues of concern to care home owners will provide a reference point for all health and safety matters. The chapters have been written in a way in which allows easy reference to be made to areas of concern.

3   The guidance contained in this booklet is *not* mandatory. Although it sets out information on the responsibilities of employers and employees under health and safety legislation, the advice on implementing safe systems of work is guidance *only*, aimed at helping care home proprietors and others meet their health and safety obligations. Employers may of course take alternative effective steps if they wish.

4   This booklet does not include guidance on fire safety. These matters are dealt with in the booklet 'Draft Guide to Fire Precautions in Residential Care Premises'[1] which is available from the Fire and Emergency Planning Department, Home Office, Queen Anne's Gate, London, SW11 9AT. Advice on fire safety may also be obtained from the Local Fire Prevention Officer.

5   The responsibilities of care home owners are the subject of a range of legislation and regulations and this is enforced by a number of different authorities.

(a)   The Health and Safety Executive (HSE) is responsible for developing health and safety standards nationally and for the inspection and enforcement of health and safety legislation in all nursing homes and residential care homes owned by local authorities.

(b)   The Environmental Health Department of the local authority is responsible for;

(i)   enforcement of health and safety legislation in private and voluntary owned residential care homes;

(ii)   food safety and hygiene enforcement action in all residential care and nursing homes.

(c)   The Registration and Inspection Unit of the Social Services Department of the local authority is responsible for the registration and inspection of residential care homes in England and Wales, or the local authority Social Work Department in Scotland.

(d)   The District Health Authority in England and Wales or the Health Boards in Scotland are responsible for registration and inspection of nursing homes.

All the above will give advice on matters relating to their particular area of concern. However, this guidance provides advice on items (a) and (b)(i) above *only*.

Legal duties

Duties of employers to employees

6 Employers have a general duty under the Health and Safety at Work etc Act 1074 to ensure, so far as is reasonably practicable, the health, safety and welfare at work of all their employees. This duty includes:

(a) providing and maintaining plant, machinery and systems of work that are safe and without risks to health;

(b) ensuring that articles and substances are used, handled, stored and transported safely and without risks to health;

(c) providing the necessary information, instruction, training and supervision to ensure the health and safety at work of all employees;

(d) maintaining a workplace that is safe and without risks to health, including safe entrance and exit; and

(e) providing and maintaining a working environment which is safe, without risks to health and with adequate welfare facilities and arrangements for employees' welfare at work.

Consultation with employees

7 Good health and safety cannot be achieved without the co-operation of employees. The role of the safety representative is therefore a valuable way of communicating with employees and also in helping managers to identify and tackle problems. If they are appointed by a recognised trade union, safety representatives have statutory rights, for example, to be consulted on matters affecting health and safety; to carry out inspections; and to request the setting up of a safety committee.

Health and safety records and documentation

8 Employers with five or more employees are required to:

(a) prepare a written statement of their general policy, organisation and arrangements for the health and safety at work of their employees. The statement and any revision of it should be brought to the attention of all the employees. Helpful guidance is available including a 'skeleton statement' which can be filled in by small employers (see Appendix 1);

(b) record significant findings of their risk assessment. This record should represent an effective statement of hazards and risks which then leads management to take the relevant actions to protect health and safety; and

(c) record their arrangements for health and safety.

9 These duties are supplemented by a wide variety of more specific regulations made under the Act. Together they form a network of legal requirements designed to achieve the main objective set out in section 2 of the Act.

Duties of employers to people not in their employment

10 Employers and self-employed people have a responsibility for the health and safety of members of the public, self-employed people or contractors' employees working with them who may be affected by work activities under their control. In fact, employers who share their workplace with another employer or self-employed person or who have other employers' staff working in their workplace, have a duty to co-operate and exchange information on health and safety.

Duties of self-employed people

11 Self-employed people have a specific duty not to create risks to the health and safety of other people or themselves. They also have other duties similar to those for employers.

Duties of people in charge of premises

12 If non-domestic premises are made available to non-employees as a place of work where they may use plant or substances provided for their use there, then the person in control of the premises has a duty to ensure that the premises and any plant or substances provided in those premises (eg the use of a greenhouse by an employee of a grounds maintenance contractor or the use of the home's ladder by a window cleaner) do not create a risk to health and safety. The extent of the responsibilities of individuals depends on how far they control the premises. (A local authority enforcement officer from the local Environmental Health Department will be able to give advice.)

Duties of employees

13 The legal duties of employees include:

(a) taking reasonable care of their own health and safety and that of others who may be affected by what they do or omit to do at work;

(b) co-operating with their employer on health and safety matters;

(c) not interfering with or misusing anything provided in the interests of health, safety and welfare of themselves or others; and

(d) informing their employer of any shortcoming in the health and safety arrangements, even when no immediate dangers exist.

14 Not all health and safety regulations are relevant to all types of work activity. However, the Management of Health and Safety Regulations 1992 *do* apply to all work activities. They put further detail on those duties of employers, the self-employed and employees mentioned above. In effect, they make much clearer what is required to comply with the general duties of the Act itself. There is also a range of approved codes of practice and other guidance to help employers understand how to carry out their duties; and these are listed where relevant.

Contractors

15 All contractors hired to work on residential care home premises, whether they are gardeners, window cleaners or builders, have their own duties to comply with health and safety legislation. However, they may need to be given information about the premises to ensure their safety, eg whether asbestos is present. Employers should enquire about the contractors own procedures so that they will not endanger themselves or resident staff. Where possible, contractors should work in an area segregated from the normal running of the home.

Health, safety and welfare of residents

16 Residential care homes differ from other work-places because not only are they a place of work but, for many people, they are home. Therefore, in meeting legal duties particularly those to non-employees, there should be a recognition of the need to maintain a homely, non-institutionalised environment.

17 People in residential care homes will have various degrees of dependence and therefore differing needs. It is undesirable to set down strict guidelines across this range. A person living in a rehabilitation hostel for alcoholics will have different requirements from an elderly person. This will be reflected in the design of the home, for example, where residents are able bodied there will be no need to provide a lift or grab rails. Having a flexible approach should not be seen as a lowering of standards, but rather that it will lead to more relevant and appropriate provision tailored to the needs of different groups.

18 Residents should be offered as much choice as possible about the way they run their lives even when this involves risk to themselves. It is normal for people to take responsible risks and people living in a residential care home are entitled to do the same. For example, being allowed to go shopping or to the local pub. Being overprotective towards residents may result in undermining their personal rights. Residents who feel competent to undertake certain activities should be free to do so. However, the emphasis is on the word 'responsible', and residents should have good information on which to base such decisions and should not endanger others.

19 The registration and inspection unit of the Social Services Department in England and Wales or the Social Work Department in Scotland will be able to give further advice on the welfare of residents.

Management of health and safety

20 Good standards of health and safety in the workplace do not happen of their own accord. For example, safe systems of work have to be implemented, staff have to be trained and machinery and equipment maintained in good condition. In other words, health and safety has to be managed, as with any other part of the business.

21 The attention paid to health and safety is not only a legal duty but makes good economic sense. Employers can ill-afford the loss of a valuable member of staff with back pain caused by poor lifting technique or an injury resulting from a preventable fall.

22 Many aspects of running a residential care home involve taking decisions which can affect health and safety. An assessment of the risks that may be present plays a major role in those decisions. The Management of Health and Safety at Work Regulations 1992 require employers to assess the risks to employees and any others who may be affected by their undertaking[2]. The assessments should be seen as a means of arriving at the right decision on how to control a risk. They are not an end in themselves and in many cases measures to control the risk can be obvious and easy to implement. Trivial risks can usually be ignored as can risks arising from routine activities associated with life in general (unless the work activity is especially relevant to those risks). The value of an assessment is in allowing all the relevant factors to be considered and thereby arriving at a better

decision. Some assessments may be simple and arise directly from observation, for example whether the lift door closes too quickly. Others may be more complex and could include:

(a) staff training needs;

(b) types of equipment, how it is used by whom; and

(c) adaptation of premises to meet needs of residents, risks to staff, residents, visitors, etc as a result of contractors working at the premises.

23 Specific risk assessments already carried out under other health and safety legislation, eg COSHH and manual handling regulations, do not need to be repeated or duplicated; they will form part of the overall risk assessment.

24 Recording significant risks gives management the opportunity of assessing how well the risks are controlled.

25 Appropriate arrangements should be considered for putting into practice the preventive and protective measures that follow from the risk assessment. Effective health and safety arrangements will cover planning, organisation, control, monitoring and review.

26 Keeping records is in some cases a legal requirement and in others a convenient and sensible way to manage health and safety. The following list could be considered when deciding which areas of activity need to be reviewed:

(a) maintenance and service records for all equipment and machines;

(b) maintenance and service records for the central heating system;

(c) lift examination records;

(d) electrical equipment and installation certificates;

(e) staff training records;

(f) accident/incident records;

(g) specific assessments: COSHH (Control of Substances Hazardous to Health) - see paragraphs 55-65, protective clothing, manual handling;

(h) in-house or self audit inspection records;

(i) drugs and medicines records;

(j) emergency lighting and fire safety records.

27 If records are kept, they will need to be accurate, up to date and retrievable. The Registered Homes Act 1984 requires that some of the above records are available for inspection. Information on this point can be obtained from the local authority Registration and Inspection Unit.

28 Monitoring the operation of the safety policy is one way of ensuring that procedures are being adhered to. Investigations of injuries and near misses will identify the need for improved management controls and can give useful information on how to prevent a recurrence. An accident investigation may show that a change of procedure is necessary.

Staff training

29 The Management of Health and Safety at Work Regulations 1992 require employers to take into account their employees' capabilities as regards health and safety when giving them tasks to do, for example previous training, knowledge and experience[2]. The employer should also ensure employees are provided with adequate health and safety training.

30 Training is an important way of achieving health and safety competence and helps to convert information into safe working practices.

31 New employees (including temporary staff) should receive induction training on health and safety, including arrangements for first aid, emergency procedures, fire and evacuation. The needs of young workers should also be given particular attention but training is needed at all levels, including top management.

32 Risk assessments should identify where specific training is required. Training needs may change when:

(a) employees transfer or take on new responsibilities, or where staff return to work after extended absence; or

(b) there is a change in equipment and systems of work or procedures.

33   The competence of staff should be monitored where lack of job knowledge and skills could adversely affect health and safety, and, if necessary, providing updated or refresher training. Special attention may need to be given to employees who deputise for others. Their skills are likely to be underdeveloped and they may need more help in understanding the health and safety issues.

34   Staff who work nightshifts also have training needs and can easily be overlooked. Accidents and ill-health can often be traced to poorly informed decisions. Training can improve job performance and it is sensible to keep a record of significant training events.

35   Competence based qualifications for a wide range of jobs in the care sector are available and accredited by the National Council for Vocational Qualifications (NVQ) and the Scottish Vocational Education Council (SCOTVEC). The units which make up the qualifications may be useful in identifying training needs including health and safety training needs.

Incidents

36 The Reporting of Injuries, Diseases and Dangerous Occurrences Regulations 1985 (RIDDOR) require employers, people in control of premises, and in some cases the self-employed, to report certain types of injury, occupational ill-health and dangerous occurrences to their enforcing authority. In the case of private and voluntary run residential care homes the enforcing authority is the local environmental health department, for nursing homes and local authority owned residential care homes it is HSE.

37 The following paragraphs give a summary of the requirements, but are by no means a comprehensive or exhaustive statement of law. More detailed information is provided in the HSE booklet HS(R)23 *Guide to the Reporting of Injuries, Diseases and Dangerous Occurrences Regulations 1985*[3].

Notification of injuries and dangerous occurrences

38 There are two ways in which injuries and incidents have to be reported to an enforcing authority and these depend on the severity and the potential for harm:

(a)   (i)   if **someone** dies or suffers a specified injury (see paragraph 39) in an accident arising from or in connection with work, or

(ii)   there is a dangerous occurrence (see paragraph 40),

then the employer should notify the enforcing authority immediately by the quickest practicable means, normally by telephone, and within seven days send a written report using form F2508 (see Appendix 5). Reports are required whether or not the person concerned is an employee;

(b)   where an employee is off work or cannot carry out their normal duties for more than three consecutive days as a result of an accident at work, this is also reportable and the employer has seven days in which to send a report to the enforcing authority.

Specified injuries

39 Injuries which are required to be notified by the quickest practicable means (see paragraph 38) are:

(a)   fracture of the skull, spine or pelvis;

(b)   fracture of any bone in the arm or wrist, but not a bone in the hand; or in the leg or ankle, but not a bone in the foot;

(c)   amputation of a hand or foot, or a finger, thumb or toe, or any part of these if the joint or bone is completely severed;

(d)   the loss of sight of an eye, a penetrating injury to an eye, or a chemical or hot metal burn to an eye;

(e)   either injury (including burns) requiring immediate medical treatment, or loss of consciousness resulting in either case from an electric shock from any electrical circuit or equipment, whether or not due to direct contact, ie contact with exposed hazardous live parts or conductors or with parts made hazardous-live due to a fault;

(f) loss of consciousness resulting from lack of oxygen;

(g) either acute illness requiring treatment, or loss of consciousness, resulting in either case from absorption of any substance by inhalation, ingestion or through the skin;

(h) acute illness requiring medical treatment where there is reason to believe that this resulted from exposure to a pathogen or infected material.

(i) any other injury which results in the person injured being admitted immediately into hospital for more than 24 hours.

Dangerous occurrences

40 Certain dangerous occurrences are required to be reported and a full list is given in the booklet HS(R) 23[3]. The most relevant to residential care homes are:

(a) the collapse of, the overturning of or the failure of any lift, hoist of mobile powered access platform;

(b) explosion, collapse or bursting of any closed vessel, including a boiler or boiler tube, in which the internal pressure was above or below atmospheric pressure, which might have been liable to cause the death of, or injuries to any person or which resulted in the stoppage of the plant involved for more than 24 hours;

(c) electrical short circuit or overload attended by fire or explosion which resulted in the stoppage of the plant

involved for more than 24 hours and might have been liable to cause death or injuries to any person;

(d) an explosion or fire occurring in any plant or place which resulted in the stoppage of that plant or suspension of normal work in that place for more than 24 hours, where such explosion or fire was due to the ignition of process materials, their by-products (including waste) or finished process;

(e) a collapse or partial collapse of any scaffold which is more than five metres high;

(f) any unintended collapse or partial collapse of:

(i) any building or structure under construction, reconstruction, alteration or demolition involving a fall of more than five tonnes of material; or

(ii) any floor or wall of any building being used as a place of work, not being a building under construction, reconstruction, alteration or demolition.

Notification of reportable diseases

41 Where a person at work suffers from a reportable disease and the work involves a specified activity, the employer should immediately send a written report to the enforcing authority. This will be required only if the employer receives a written diagnosis of the disease made by a doctor; and the ill employee's current job involves a specified work activity.

The reportable disease and specified work activities which are most likely to affect the residential care sector are:

(a) **hepatitis** - work involving exposure to human blood products or body secretions and excretions; and

(b) **tuberculosis** - work with people or with any other material which might be a source of infection.

42 Although not reportable under RIDDOR, the Environmental Health Department should be notified if any person (particularly food handlers) is suspected or confirmed as having food poisoning.

Reporting in writing

43 Form F2508 should be used to report injuries and dangerous occurrences, form F2508A should be used for cases of disease. Appendices 5 and 6 reproduce the forms and these may be photocopied for your own use. Alternatively they can be purchased from HSE Books (see back cover). Authorised report forms generated by a computerised accident recording system, several of which are commercially available, may also be used.

Record keeping

44 The employer should keep a record of any reportable accident and dangerous occurrence. These records should include:

(a) date and time of accident or occurrence;

(b) name, occupation and nature of injury of person affected;

(c) place where incident happened; and

(d) a brief description of the circumstances.

The employer should also keep a record of any reportable disease. These records should include:

(a) date of diagnosis of the disease;

(b) occupation of the person affected;

(c) name or nature of the disease.

These records must be kept for at least three years.

RIDDOR and non-RIDDOR accidents

45 Figure 1 shows a table of typical accidents and gives details of whether or not they are reportable under RIDDOR.

46 With all incidents, if in doubt report them, incidents which are not reportable will be filtered out by the enforcing authority.

47 The duty to report injuries, diseases and dangerous occurrences is placed on the person who will either be the employer or the person for the time being having control of the premises. In order for the incident to be reportable, an incident must arise out of or in connection with a work activity.

48 Reporting an incident does not suggest in any way that you accept responsibility for the event or that an offence has been committed; it is simply informing the enforcing authority that an incident has occurred at your premises. Failure to report a

Figure 1 RIDDOR and non-RIDDOR accidents

Person Involved	Accident Details	Type of Injury	Reportable under RIDDOR
Employee	Fell off step ladder while cleaning cupboard in care home. Sustained broken arm	Major injury	Phone enforcing authority. Send F2508 within 7 days
Employee	Hurt back while lifting resident out of bath. Off work for 5 days	Over-3-day injury	Send F2508 within 7 days to enforcing authority
Employee	Hurt back while digging garden at home (employee's home). Off work for 5 days		Not reportable. Accident not at work
Employee	Banged head on door at work. Taken to hospital. Detained for 24 hours. Returned to work next day	Major injury	Phone enforcing authority. Send F2508 within 7 days
Resident	Tripped over vacuum cleaner and broke leg	Major injury	Phone enforcing authority. Send F2508 within 7 days
Resident	Died in sleep		Not reportable if natural causes
Resident	Found on bedroom floor with broken leg		Not reportable providing no additional factors, eg worn carpets
Employee	Driver twisted ankle while assisting resident out of vehicle. Unable to drive for 4 days but assists in home with light duties	Over-3-day injury	Send F2508 within 7 days to enforcing authority
Part time employee	Normally works Mon-Wed. Injured back while lifting resident on Monday. Absent Tuesday and Wednesday. On return to work the following Monday reports that injury did not abate until Friday	Over-3-day injury	Send F2508 within 7 days to enforcing authority
Visitor	Tripped over frayed carpet. Broke arm	Major injury	Phone enforcing authority. Send F2508 within 7 days
Employee	Bitten by a resident. Off work for 4 days	Over-3-day	Send F2508 to enforcing authority within 7 days

reportable injury, dangerous occurrence or disease described in RIDDOR is a criminal offence and may result in prosecution.

Notification of accidents to the Registration and Inspection Unit

49 Accidents and dangerous occurrences reportable under RIDDOR should not be confused with those which may be reportable to other authorities. Certain accidents have to be reported under other legislation. Further advice on this point can be obtained from the Registration and Inspection Unit of the Social Services Department in England and Wales or the Social Work Department in Scotland.

Occupational health

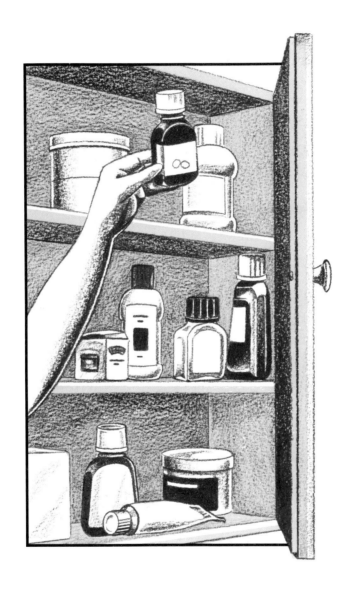

First aid

50 Under the Health and Safety (First Aid) Regulations 1981 workplaces should have first aid provision. The form it should take depends on various factors, including the nature and degree of the hazards at work, whether there is shift working, what medical services are available, and the number of employees. The HSE booklet *First aid at work*[4] contains an Approved Code of Practice and guidance notes to help employers meet their obligations.

51 The minimum requirement for any workplace is that at all times when people are at work (including night shifts), there should be at least one appointed person who will take charge in an emergency situation, eg by calling an ambulance. Ideally, it is recommended that an appointed person should have received emergency first-aid training.

52 Although the Regulations refer only to facilities for employees, employers may wish to extend these to cover residents and give consideration to providing a qualified first aider.

53 A first-aid box should be provided and should contain only items that a first aider has been trained to use. It should not contain medication of any kind. It should be kept adequately stocked. Where there is a known incidence of Hepatitis B, additional items, for example disposable rubber gloves, should be provided.

54 All cases dealt with should be recorded by the first aider or appointed person. Records should include at least the name of the casualty, date, time and circumstances of the accident with details of the injury sustained and any treatment given. Employees or their representatives may wish to inspect these records at any time, they should therefore be kept in a suitable place rendering them easily available for inspection.

Control of Substances Hazardous to Health Regulations (COSHH) 1988

55 The Control of Substances Hazardous to Health Regulations 1988 (COSHH)[5] require employers to prevent or control exposure to hazardous substances at work. The Regulations were introduced to ensure that any exposure to hazardous substances at work is prevented, or where this is not reasonably practicable, adequately controlled. This responsibility on an employer applies to the protection of any person who may be affected by the hazardous substance, and not just their employees.

56 The employer is required to carry out an assessment of the health risks faced by their employees, and to state the action they intend to take to prevent, or control the exposure of their workforce to hazardous substances. In addition, the risk to residents' health from exposure to substances used in the residential home should be addressed in the assessment.

57   Substances that are hazardous to health include substances which are very toxic, toxic, harmful, irritant or corrosive. In a residential care home, cleaning materials such as disinfectants, detergents, polish and dishwasher products are widely used. Some of these may be hazardous substances and may create a risk to health if improperly used or mixed together.

58   The Regulations also include harmful micro-organisms (and thus cover clinical waste and soiled laundry) and substantial quantities of dust and indeed any material, mixture or compound used at work, or arising from work activities, which can harm people's health.

59   The Regulations require all employers to:

(a)   Assess the risk to their employees and others from exposure to hazardous substances at work and so establish whether precautions are needed.

(b)   Introduce appropriate measures to prevent or control the risk for those substances where a risk has been identified which needs to be controlled.

(c)   Ensure that control measures are used and that equipment is properly maintained and procedures observed.

(d)   Where necessary, monitor the exposure of the workers and carry out an appropriate form of surveillance of their health.

(e)   Inform, instruct and train employees about the risks and the precautions to be taken.

COSHH assessment

60   Employers should look at the work activities and determine:

(a)   What substances are present and in what form?

(b)   What harmful effects are possible?

(c)   Where and how the substances are actually used or handled?

(d)   Whether harmful substances are given off or produced?

(e)   Whether a safer substitute material can be used?

(f)   Who could be affected, to what extent, for how long and under what circumstances?

(g)   How likely is it that exposure will happen?

(h)   Are precautions required, such as protective clothing?

61   Certain information about products may be found on the label. If the information is not readily available from the label or suppliers advisory leaflet, then a data sheet for that product may be obtained from the supplier or manufacturer. They have a legal duty to supply such information. Many proprietary cleaning materials contain risk phrases such as 'avoid contact with skin'. In these circumstances, information from the COSHH assessment would be used to make staff aware of the risk, suitable training/instruction would then be given on how to use the product safely and, where appropriate, protective gloves provided and staff instructed to wear them.

62 The assessment will normally need to be written down for those substances which are hazardous to health. The assessment does not require all substances used in the workplace to be listed, eg soap, ink etc.

63 Some chemicals which are relatively harmless on their own may become extremely hazardous when mixed, for example toilet cleaner and bleach may react together and give off harmful fumes. It is important that the employees are made aware of potential hazards.

64 Where health and safety information is contained on a label, the contents should not be decanted into smaller containers unless fully labelled in line with the original.

65 As with all management tasks, the process should be kept under review to ensure that the appropriate control measures are being carried out and to check whether there have been any significant changes to working procedures, new materials, etc which would merit reassessment.

Accident case

■ There have been two deaths in residential care homes due to residents mistaking cleaning fluids for a drink. In both cases the fluid had been decanted into an unmarked container.

Clinical waste

66 Staff employed in residential care homes may have to deal with body fluids and wastes which are potentially hazardous to the handler. Clinical waste falls within the scope of the Control of Substances Hazardous to Health Regulations 1988 (COSHH). All clinical waste is divided into five categories - Groups A to E.

■ **Group A** All human tissue including blood (whether infected or not). Waste materials where the assessment indicates a risk to staff handling them, for example from infectious disease cases; soiled surgical dressings, swabs and other soiled waste.

■ **Group B** Discarded syringe needles, cartridges, broken glass and any other contaminated disposable sharp instruments or items.

■ **Group C** Microbiological cultures and waste from pathology departments and research laboratories.

■ **Group D** Certain pharmaceutical products and chemical wastes (includes out of date pharmaceuticals).

■ **Group E** Items used to dispose of urine, faeces and other bodily secretions or excretions assessed as not falling within Group A. This includes used disposable bed pans, or bed pan liners, incontinence pads, stoma bags and urine containers.

67 Group E is the most relevant to residential care with Groups A and B to a lesser extent. Group E contains items which will usually present a low level of risk. However, as the actual risk cannot be readily demonstrated, items within this group should be treated as clinical waste. While the risk may be low, the waste from this group will often be of an offensive nature. It is therefore advisable that adequate procedures are put into effect for proper handling and disposal arrangements.

68 Procedures for handling clinical waste should include:

Identification of categories of clinical waste

Clear information, instruction and training should be provided for all persons who work in areas where clinical waste arises.

Means of segregation

Colour coded containers or sacks should be used (see table).

COLOUR	TYPE OF WASTE
Yellow	Groups A and B - incineration only. Also Group E.
Yellow with black stripes	Group E - waste suitable for landfill.
Black	Normal household waste

Disposable plastic coloured sacks may be used for Groups A and E and should meet the standards of BS 6642, or where there is a harmonised European standard. The sacks should only be filled to three-quarters full and then sealed by tying off the neck.

Group B, including broken glass, should be put into sharps containers. Syringes should be disposed of intact. When three quarters full, the containers should be sealed. Used needles should not be disposed of in domestic waste. The containers used should be specifically designed for sharps in accordance with BS 7320, or where there is a harmonised European standard. On no account should soft drink cans, plastic bottles or similar containers be used for disposal of needles since these could present serious hazards to disposal staff if they were to be disposed of in domestic waste. Sharps containers should not be placed in bags prior to disposal.

Storage

An area should be provided for the clinical waste prior to collection. It should be:

(a)   reserved for clinical waste only;

(b)   secure, totally enclosed and sited on a well-drained, impervious, hard-standing surface;

(c)   easily accessible to authorised persons;

(d)   kept secure from entry by animals, rodents and insects;

(e)   sited away from food areas and routes used by the public; and

(f)   well-lit and ventilated.

Separate storage for sharps containers with a higher degree of security may be required, particularly if collection frequencies are likely to be greater than weekly.

Training

All employees who are required to handle and move clinical waste should be adequately trained in safe procedures and in dealing with spillages or other incidents. Refresher training will also be required. Records of training should be kept. Training should normally include:

(a)   risks associated with clinical waste (basic personal hygiene);

(b)   segregation and storage;

(c)   procedures for dealing with spillages and accidents; and

(d)   use of protective clothing.

Accidents and incidents

The employer should identify procedures for dealing with accidents and incidents involving clinical waste. This should include:

(a)   appropriate first aid measures;

(b)   prompt and formal reporting procedure;

(c)   recording of accident or incident; and

(d)   investigation and implementation of remedial action.

Spillages

The procedure laid down for clinical waste should specify how spillages can be cleaned up safely, including decontamination of the affected area. Appropriate protective clothing should be specified.

Disposal of waste

Safe disposal of clinical waste is the responsibility of the residential care home owner. Large quantities of clinical waste should not be allowed to accumulate. Arrangements for disposal should be of sufficient frequency to prevent large quantities accumulating. The domestic waste collection service should not be used for clinical waste. The options for disposal are:

(a)   local authority special collection and disposal service for clinical waste;

(b)   independent contractor to local hospital incinerator;

(c)   independent contractor to local authority facilities; and

(d)   independent contractor to contractor's incinerator.

69   Contractors who incinerate clinical waste can be asked to certify incineration. Such certificates should be retained for a reasonable period. Local waste regulation authorities can give advice on disposal, including details of facilities available locally.

Blood-borne infections

70   To minimise the risk of contamination from blood-borne viruses, contact with blood should be avoided. Staff with cuts or other open wounds should cover them before commencing work and a waterproof dressing should be used. Good hygiene practices include: using disposable equipment whenever possible; keeping everything clean (floors and surfaces regularly washed, carpets vacuumed); disinfecting work surfaces contaminated with blood; and encouraging employees to routinely wash their hands.

71 Consideration should be given to providing information to employees on what to do in the event of body fluid spillages. Advice is available from the local Environmental Health Department. In homes where there is known to be a high incidence of Hepatitis B amongst residents, staff should be encouraged to be immunised, especially where those residents have unpredictable behaviour. Unvaccinated staff should not be asked to carry out duties where risks are seen to be greater, ie clearing body fluid spills where the virus is known to be present. A needlestick policy may need to be implemented, depending on the requirements of Local Health Authority policy. A needlestick policy should also cover other blood-borne viruses such as HIV and Hepatitis B.

Drugs and medicines

72 Drugs and medicines can be dangerous if misused. All drugs should therefore be correctly labelled and procedures should be adopted to ensure safe stock control. Drugs should be kept in a secure location to prevent misuse and unauthorised access.

73 Further advice may be obtained from your pharmacist or the Registration and Inspection Unit of the

Social Services Department in England and Wales or the Social Work Department in Scotland.

Asbestos

74 In older premises, asbestos may be present in a variety of forms in such places as boiler rooms and in such structures as fire-resistant partitioning. If the presence of asbestos is suspected, specialist help may be required to establish the nature of the material, and the risks it may pose. Asbestos in situ should not normally create a risk unless work has to be done which could disturb it, or it has been damaged and asbestos fibres could be released into the air. When asbestos exists in a building the options to be considered are usually: leave the material in place effectively sealed; leave the material in place unsealed (providing that if left unsealed it does not create a risk to health); or remove and dispose of the asbestos (this option should normally only be considered if the asbestos is in a very poor condition or major renovation work is being completed). Again, expert help may be required to decide which option is the most appropriate.

75 If asbestos containing materials have to be removed, first seek the advice of the local Environmental Health Department or the local HSE area office as the work will have to be done by a licensed contractor. When maintenance or other work has to be done which could disturb asbestos containing material, or involve direct work upon it, any contractor doing the work should be informed of its presence. Extensive published guidance is available from HSE on work with asbestos, and from the Department of Environment on asbestos materials to be found in buildings.

76 Where asbestos insulation material is concealed in any lagging and door panels etc, information on its existence should be provided to employees. The appropriate use of labels is recommended.

Water temperatures

Legionnaires' disease

77 Legionnaires' disease is a type of pneumonia which may also have serious effects on other organs of the body. Infection is caused by inhaling airborne droplets or particles containing viable legionella. Most reported cases have occurred in the 40 to 70 year age group. Although healthy individuals may develop legionnaires' disease, people thought to be at an enhanced risk of infection include smokers, alcoholics, and patients with cancer, chronic respiratory or kidney disease. Residential care homes are likely to contain a high proportion of susceptible people.

78 The ecology of legionella in water systems is not fully understood. However, water temperatures in the range of 20 to 45°C favour growth; it is uncommon to find proliferation below 20°C, and it does not survive above 60°C. Therefore, water services should operate at temperatures that prevent the proliferation of legionella, ie:

   (a) hot water storage (calorifiers) - 60°C;

   (b) hot water distribution, at least 50°C attainable at the taps within one minute of running;

   (c) cold water storage and distribution - 20°C or below.

79 Further guidance is available on the prevention and control of legionella in the HSE booklets *The control of legionellosis (including legionnaires' disease)*[6] and the Approved Code of Practice *The prevention or control of legionellosis (including legionnaires' disease)*[7].

Scalding

80 At water temperatures above 50°C there is a danger of scalding which increases with temperature. The risk is great to persons who are elderly and those with sensory loss.

81 It is recommended that the temperature should not exceed 43°C where hot water outlets are accessible to residents and workers. Where there is total body immersion, consideration should be given to installing thermostatic mixers with fail safe devices, ie those which automatically close the hot water supply if the cold supply fails. At hand wash basins, one method of reducing the risk of scalding is to provide single lever or control mechanical mixers starting from cold with a tamperproof stop to limit full hot water flow.

82 A simple test may be carried out on mixing devices to ensure that they operate safety, ie the hot water flow is cut off when the cold supply is interrupted. The mixing devices may require regular maintenance and information on this is normally contained in the manufacturer's instructions.

83 Where washing and bathing facilities are used by staff only, it will not be necessary for the hot water outlet to be controlled. However, care should be taken to restrict access to residents and visitors to 'staff only' areas.

84 In rehabilitation training areas the object is to provide a near domestic environment. Blending and temperature control devices are unlikely to be needed, provided that there is adequate supervision by staff who have received information and training on the risks of scalding and safe procedures. Labelling hot water outlets with 'very hot water', will help to prevent inadvertent scalding. Other regulatory bodies may require that temperature control devices should be fitted in certain circumstances. The local authority Registration and Inspection Unit of the Social Services Department in England and Wales or the Social Work Department in Scotland may be able to provide further information on this point.

Acceptable risk

85 In deciding whether or not to fit a water temperature regulating device, an assessment should be carried out on the capabilities and needs of the residents in relation to bathing. It will be necessary to assess the risk of scalding to the residents and their right to choose to have a hot bath, if they so wish.

Surface temperatures

86 It is recommended that heated surfaces of radiators, accessible pipes or panel type convectors, and other heating devices should not exceed 43°C when the system is operating at the maximum design output.

87 The risk of burns on hot surfaces may be reduced by:

(a)   reducing the flow temperatures;

(b)   guarding the heated areas; and

(c)   providing low surface temperature heat emitters.

88 There may be other design solutions which help to ensure that the maximum surface temperatures do not exceed 43°C and help to prevent possible risks of burns.

Manual handling

89 Almost four out of every ten accidents reported in the health care sector arise from manual handling. In residential care homes there will be a range of manual handling tasks from the simple lifting of provisions to complicated lifts involving residents. Sprains and strains of backs and limbs are often sustained from manual handling. Injuries may also occur as a result of cumulative damage often sustained over a considerable period, which can result in physical impairment or even permanent disability.

90 The Manual Handling Operations Regulations 1992 are intended to reduce the large incidence of injury and disability caused by manual handling[8].

91 The Regulations require employers to follow three steps:

(a) avoid hazardous manual handling operations so far as is reasonably practicable;

(b) make a suitable and sufficient assessment of any hazardous manual handling operations that cannot be avoided; and

(c) reduce the risk of injury so far as is reasonably practicable;

Manual handling operations means any transporting or supporting of a load (including the lifting, putting down, pushing, pulling, carrying or moving) by hand or bodily force. For this purpose, 'load' includes a person.

Avoidance of manual handling

92 When a risk of injury from a manual handling operation is identified the first questions to ask are whether the operation can be eliminated altogether: is the handling operation necessary; or could the desired result be achieved in some entirely different way?

93 If a handling operation cannot be avoided entirely then a further question should be asked: can the operation be mechanised?

94 The introduction of mechanisation may create other, different risks, for example the introduction of bath hoists, can introduce risks associated with the equipment and requiring separate precautions.

95 Where the initial appraisal shows that a manual handling operation may involve a significant risk of injury, then a suitable and sufficient assessment should be undertaken.

96 The assessment should be recorded unless:

(a) it could very easily be repeated and explained at any time because it is simple and obvious; or

(b) the manual handling operation is quite straightforward and of low risk, is going to last only a very short time, and the time taken to record it would be disproportionate.

Making an assessment

97 When making a manual handling assessment there are four elements to be considered: the task, the load, the working environment and the individual's capabilities. Schedule 1 to the Manual Handling Regulations 1992 lists the factors which should be taken into account when making an assessment. See Appendix 7 for further information. It should be possible to complete the majority of assessments in-house. The guidance on the regulations will help when this task is undertaken.

Reducing the risk of injury

98 Once the assessment has been made and the areas of risk identified, reasonably practicable steps should be taken to reduce the risk of injury.

The task

Improving task layout

99 The optimum position for storage of loads is around waist height; storage much above or below this height should ideally be reserved for easily handled loads or loads that are handled infrequently.

Using the body more efficiently

100 Equipment may be used to reduce or remove the need for twisting, stooping and stretching. It should not be assumed that because a particular manual handling operation has always been undertaken that it is unavoidable, for example carrying laundry when a trolley could be used.

101 Where there is a risk of injury to staff from lifting residents in and out of the bath, consideration should be given to using bath hoists. Careful selection of suitable hoists can improve the residents' independence and dignity.

Improving the work routine

102 Fatigue increases the likelihood of manual handling injuries, therefore the number and length of rest or recovery periods are important. Work should be organised so that, where practicable, manual handling tasks are spread throughout the working shift. This allows staff longer recovery periods between the manual handling activities. Staffing levels will affect workloads and rest and recovery periods.

Team handling

103 Where a handling operation would be difficult or unsafe for one person, handling by a team of two or more may provide an answer. However, team handling may introduce other risks which the assessment should consider.

Personal protective equipment

104 The nature of the load may necessitate the use of personal protective equipment such as gloves, aprons and overalls to prevent contamination, for example when handling soiled laundry or clinical waste. Care should be taken to ensure that the wearing of personal protective equipment does not impair an individual's ability to carry out the manual handling task, either by impeding the hold on the load or by constraining posture.

Maintenance and accessibility of equipment

105 All equipment used for manual handling (including personal protective equipment) should be well-maintained. This would normally involve a system for reporting and correcting defects. Handling equipment and aids that are not readily accessible are less likely to be used fully and effectively.

The load

106 Human beings and inanimate loads vary in terms of size, weight, shape, fragility, stability etc, but human beings display different characteristics. They can help (or hinder) the manual handling operation; they may feel pain and anxiety and may suffer from inappropriate handling, they have personal dignity and they are irreplaceable.

107 Some residents may become violent or agitated when lifted or handled, others although willing to assist at the start of a lift may suddenly find themselves unable to continue. The response by the handlers may determine whether injury to themselves or the resident is avoided. Training for staff on how to deal with such situations, may help to prevent possible injury. A natural reaction, while assisting a resident to walk for example, is to try to prevent

them from falling and injuries have occurred to both staff and residents in such circumstances. Properly positioned, the helper may either be able to prevent a fall or allow a controlled fall and having made the resident comfortable, determine whether another person or a mechanical aid should be used to move the resident.

For loads, other than people, consideration should be given to making them lighter, smaller or easier to manage, easier to grasp, more stable, and less damaging to hold.

The working environment

108 Manual handling tasks are often made easier by good design. When considering new or replacement equipment such as sinks, sluices, catering and laundry equipment and storage areas etc, working heights can be chosen to alleviate handling risks. Employees are often required to lift buckets of water in and out of sinks fixed at a high level. Providing low level sinks may help to prevent the risk of back injuries. Raising the height of laundry equipment by placing it on a platform can also assist the laundry workers. The working height of many items of furniture can be varied, for example bed heights. High beds and chairs are generally easier for people who are physically dependent to get in and out of, thus reducing the need for assistance from staff.

109 Some simple measures can be taken to reduce the amount of handling by care assistants and increase the independence of the resident:

(a) provision of grab rails at strategic heights adjacent to the bath;

(b) provision of a vertical pole extending from floor to ceiling adjacent to and half way along the bath;

(c) provision of a bath-bench and seat. The bench should fit across the width of the bath and may protrude if supported. The seat is fitted inside the bath and to the front of the bench;

(d) provision of a walk-in shower with a seat.

These aids can be easily fitted in small bathrooms where space is at a premium.

Individual capabilities

Personal capacity

110 Particular consideration should be given to employees who are or have been recently pregnant or who are known to have injuries or ill-health etc. In general the lifting strength of women as a group is less than that of men but there is considerable overlap; some women can deal safely with greater loads than some men.

Knowledge and training

111 The manual handling operation should be designed, where possible, to suit individuals, rather than the other way round. Effective training has an important part to play in reducing the risk of manual handling injury, but is not a substitute for improving the task, the load and the working environment, as appropriate.

112 Special techniques will probably be required for lifting residents. They will depend on the situation and the ability of the resident. Care should be taken to avoid tender and painful areas. Specialist advice may need to be sought on how to help residents in and out of the bath, from bed to chair, how to lift a resident from the floor after a fall, how to assist a resident walking, and any other situation where a care assistant may have to help a resident. Groups such as the Royal Society for the Prevention of Accidents (RoSPA), the Ergonomics Society, the Chartered Society of Physiotherapists and the National Back Pain Association will be able to give further advice on all aspects of lifting. There are many information and training packs available, but care should be taken when selecting these to ensure that they are suitable and relevant to your particular home, taking into account the needs of staff and residents.

113 Clothing, including protective clothing and uniforms, is another factor which has a direct impact on the ease of movement and ability to achieve appropriate posture. Clothing should be well-fitting and restrict movement as little as possible.

General working environment

114 The Workplace (Health, Safety and Welfare) Regulations 1992 require employers, where appropriate, to reduce the risks associated with work in or near buildings[9]. Premises that are built after the 1 January 1993, or existing premises that are modified, extended or converted, will be required to comply with the Regulations. All other premises will be required to comply from 1 January 1996. These Regulations give more detail to the general duties of employers under the Health and Safety at Work etc Act 1974. They are intended to protect the health, safety and welfare of everyone in the workplace, and to ensure that adequate welfare facilities are provided for people at work. Further guidance is set out in the Approved Code of Practice *(Workplace (Health, Safety and Welfare) Regulations 1992*[9].

115 The Regulations place a wide-ranging series of duties on employers. They fall under three main headings:

(a) Initial structure of the building as it affects users (eg design of windows to allow safe cleaning).

(b) The interaction between the building, its layout and the people using it as a workplace (eg provisions for ventilation).

(c) The provision of basic facilities for employees (eg toilets, rest rooms etc).

Floors

116 Given that the majority of injuries are as a result of slips, trips and falls, particular attention should be paid to ways of reducing them. Floor coverings that are selected having regard to their slip resistance, and whenever possible are flat and free from obstructions, will help to reduce the likelihood of such accidents.

117 Holes and defects in floor coverings should be repaired, particularly those on staircases. Where immediate repair cannot be effected, it may be necessary to prevent people passing through the area by roping it off.

118 The use of strategically placed grab rails offers the resident security, especially where there are changes of floor levels.

Stairs

119 Stairs can present a hazard to everyone. Given that some residents will find climbing stairs difficult, stairs that are designed so as to reduce any risk from falls will help to alleviate the possibility of an accident occurring.

120 Stairs should be:

(a) soundly constructed;

(b) properly maintained;

(c) of adequate width with handrails on both sides of the stairway where residents lack mobility and require extra support, unless a stairlift is installed;

(d) well-lit.

121 It is advisable that stairs should not be:

(a) steep, winding, curved or have open risers;

(b) obstructed by stairlifts or any other material.

Appropriate safety measures such as locks may need to be considered for doors which open directly onto the top of a stairway.

Lighting

122 Good lighting is essential in all areas and particularly on stairs and corridors whether used by residents, staff or visitors.

123 All rooms used for principal living activities should where feasible, have good natural light. Electric lighting should be provided throughout the premises to a level adequate to enable activities to be carried out safely. Elderly people and persons with a visual handicap may require increased levels of lighting. People with hearing loss also need adequate lighting levels in order to be able

to communicate effectively. All homes should consider the need for emergency lighting.

124 Placing the main control for lighting in the premises in a secure area, will help to prevent lighting being switched off inadvertently.

Ventilation

125 Effective and suitable provision should be made to ensure that all parts of the home are ventilated by a sufficient quantity of fresh or purified air. The introduction and circulation of fresh or purified air should be at a rate sufficient to reduce stale, contaminated, hot or humid air, but should not cause discomfort.

126 In most residential care homes, suitably placed windows capable of being easily opened and closed may be sufficient for effective ventilation. For kitchens, which can be hot and humid, consideration should be given to installing mechanical exhaust ventilation.

Temperature

127 The temperature in all workplaces should be reasonable, taking account of:

(a) the work clothing worn by employees,

(b) the type of work carried out,

(c) the humidity and air movement,

(d) the outside temperature,

(e) the time of year.

Windows

128 Serious injuries have occurred when people have fallen through glass windows. It may therefore be necessary to fit suitable safety material to transparent surfaces of windows at or below waist level. These materials would include toughened or safety glass. As an alternative, a barrier may be provided to raise the effective height of the sill.

129 Windows which are open and are large enough to allow persons to fall out should be restrained sufficiently to prevent such falls. For example, double hung sash type windows can be easily and cheaply modified to reduce the size of the opening by fixing screws in the sash boxes.

130 Consideration should be given to glazing full glass doors and patio windows with toughened or safety glass conforming to BS 6262 (code of practice for glazing for buildings), or where there is a harmonised European standard. Such doors and windows should have a conspicuous mark or feature sufficiently obvious that people will be unlikely to collide with the glazing.

131 Any window alterations should be discussed with the Fire Prevention Officer.

Accident case

■ A 91 year old resident fell 15 feet from her bedroom window and died from her injuries. The window was fully openable.

Accident case

■ A 63 year old resident fell to her death from her first floor window. The window was of a hung sash type.

Doors

132 Doors should be designed so that they can easily be opened by residents. Where residents are frail, doors fitted with strong self-closers should be avoided.

133 Where doors (and gates) swing in both directions, a transparent panel should be provided except for gates which are low enough to see over.

134 Doors opening directly onto staircases, for example cellar doors, should always be kept locked, except where they are emergency exit doors.

Lifts

135 All new passenger lifts should be constructed to a suitable standard (for example BS 5655, Part 1, 1986, or Part 2, 1988, or where there is a harmonised European standard) and comply with relevant legislation.

136 Passenger lifts installed in existing homes which have been built in accordance with BS 5900, known as 'homelifts', should be upgraded where possible as recommended by HSE in the guidance leaflet *Safety of passenger lifts in private nursing/residential care homes: improving the safety of 'homelifts'*[10].

137 The lift should be thoroughly examined every six months by a competent person. The competent person would usually be an insurance company surveyor or engineer from the lift company who specialises in this work. The competent person should provide the proprietor of the home, where the lift is installed, with a record of the results of the examination of the lift. It is advised that these records are kept available for inspection at the home.

138 Some automatic doors of lifts close quickly and/or the closing mechanism is too strong for some residents, especially those who are unable to enter or leave the lift cage quickly, resulting in the resident being knocked or trapped by the door. Altering the door closing mechanism so that it closes slowly and less forcefully may help to prevent accidents.

139 The lift should be adequately maintained in accordance with the manufacturer's instructions. The manufacturer's instructions should also be followed regarding the safe and proper operation of the lift; this is particularly important with hydraulic lifts.

140 Likewise, proper use should be made of the manufacturer's advice concerning safe release of passengers from a lift car in an 'emergency' situation. At least one member of staff trained to deal with such an incident should be on the premises at all times when the lift is in use in order to rescue passengers trapped in a lift car. In the event of trained staff not being available, then the lift maintenance company should be contacted. On no account should untrained staff attempt to free passengers trapped in a lift car.

Stairlifts

141 Stairlifts should not normally be installed in new residential care homes since they are designed for use in domestic premises where only infrequent or light use of the stairlift normally occurs. However, in some circumstances they may be used in commercial premises provided that the additional features specified in BS 5776: 1979 Appendix D (or where there is a harmonised European standard) are followed, namely:

(a) stairlifts should be installed in residential care homes only in exceptional circumstances and only where it is not reasonably practicable to incorporate a passenger lift;

(b) in no circumstances should a stairlift be considered to be a suitable means of escape;

(c) before installing a stairlift, there should be full consultation with:

(i) the Fire Prevention Officer to ensure the proposal will not conflict with means of escape provisions and evacuation procedures,

(ii) the local authority environmental health department to ensure compliance with relevant health and safety requirements,

(iii)   the building control department of the local authority to ensure compliance with the relevant building regulations,

(iv)   the registration authority to ensure compliance with relevant registration requirements;

(d)   appropriate safety signs and instructions for use should be clearly displayed at each end of travel.

142 A competent person should thoroughly examine the stairlift every six months and the stairlift should be adequately maintained in accordance with the manufacturer's instructions.

143 An assessment should be carried out to ascertain whether residents are able to use the stairlift safely without assistance. Where residents require help in using the stairlift, procedures should be considered to ensure assistance is available.

Accommodation for clothing

144 Suitable and sufficient accommodation should be provided for any employees own clothing which is not worn during working hours, and for special clothing which is worn by any person at work but which is not taken home, eg overalls provided by the employer.

145 Where clothing has to be changed at work, changing facilities should be provided.

Staff rest rooms

146 New residential care homes, occupied from 1 January 1993, should have a separate rest room for the use of employees. Existing homes only need to provide a rest area. Rest rooms and rest areas should be large enough, and have sufficient chairs and tables for the number of employees likely to use them at any one time. Suitable arrangements are also necessary to protect non-smokers from discomfort caused by tobacco smoke.

Smoking in the home

147 Nowadays fewer people are smokers and attitudes to smoking are changing. There is increasing concern over the possible health effects of breathing other people's tobacco smoke - environmental tobacco smoke (ETS). Work is one of a few situations where non-smokers may have to spend long periods in close contact with smokers.

148 Employers should consider drawing up a policy to limit ETS at work. There is the added complication of the residential home not only being a workplace but also the residents' home where they should have certain freedoms as if in their own private dwelling. Full in-depth consultation with employees and residents is highly desirable for the smooth implementation of policies designed to limit exposure to ETS. A policy is very much more likely to be accepted by employees and residents if they feel they have been properly consulted.

149 An effective policy on smoking may include the following elements:

(a) allocating smokers and non-smokers separate rooms where possible;

(b) designating separate smoking and non-smoking common rooms where possible;

(c) banning smoking in all common areas such as corridors, lifts, dining room;

(d) improving ventilation so that smoke is more effectively removed from the working environment.

150 Some residents may wish to smoke in their bedrooms. The views of the Fire Prevention Officer should be sought on this matter.

Sanitary conveniences and washing facilities

151 Suitable and sufficient sanitary and washing facilities should be provided for the maximum number of persons likely to be at work at any one time. It should be possible for people to use them without undue delay.

152 In sanitary accommodation used by women, suitable means should be provided for the disposal of sanitary dressings.

153 In some smaller homes staff may have to share sanitary and washing facilities with residents. However, this should not prejudice staff use of the facilities. The number of sanitary conveniences and washing facilities should be increased if necessary.

Radon gas

154 Radon is a colourless, odourless, naturally occurring radioactive gas present in the air. It has always been possible to receive doses of radiation from radon gas. Radon originates in the ground, and can permeate to the surface. It can enter buildings from underneath and accumulate, particularly in basements and ground floor rooms. Some parts of the country are more affected than others. The counties most seriously affected are Cornwall and Devon. However, substantially increased radon levels have also been found in parts of Derbyshire, Northamptonshire, Somerset, Grampian and the Highlands of Scotland.

155 When radon decays, tiny particles are formed which can be breathed into the lung. Radiation from these particles can cause cancer, which can take many years to develop. Smoking and exposure to radon are known to work together to increase the risk of developing lung cancer.

156 Some employees in residential care homes are likely to have an increased exposure due to the time they spend at work. It may be necessary for homes in those areas that are particularly affected to take steps to determine the risks from exposure to radon, and where appropriate take adequate remedial measures.

Building construction is an important factor in controlling radon where it exists, and levels are generally lower in well-ventilated structures. When considering remedial action, it is important to take account of the increased time spent in homes compared to the typical working day in an office or factory.

Central heating systems

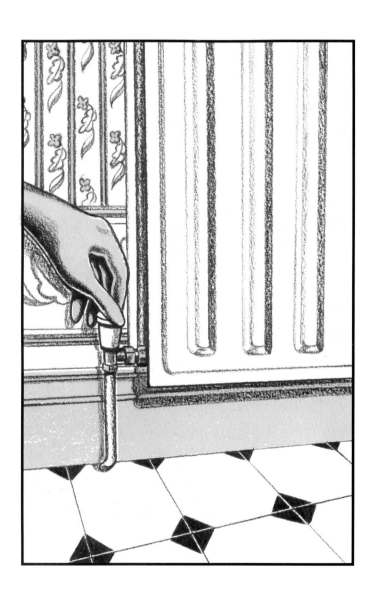

Gas safety

157 All boilers and central heating systems should be installed and serviced regularly under contract by competent persons only. In the case of gas systems, such work should only be done by businesses which are members of the Council of Registered Gas Installers (CORGI).

158 Steam boilers which are part of a central heating system, may be covered by the Pressure Systems and Transportable Gas Containers Regulations 1989.

159 Your local Environmental Health Department or the local offices of HSE can advise you on these Regulations.

Liquid petroleum gas (LPG)

160 Portable gas and paraffin heaters should not be used or allowed in residential care homes where they cannot be adequately or safely controlled. They present added risk not only of fire and burns but also of explosion, should fire break out. If they have to be used in short-term emergencies, such heaters and their safety devices should be confirmed to be in a safe working condition by a competent person before use, and then safely located away from flammable materials and means of escape. Thought should also be given to the need for supplementary fireguards, in accordance with BS 6778 where appropriate (or where there is a harmonised European standard), and means to prevent interference or accidental damage. Any spare LPG cylinders should be stored in a well-ventilated position in the open-air, away from any openings into the building, drains or gulleys.

Electrical safety

161 The use of electricity at residential care home premises is subject to the Electricity at Work Regulations 1989. The Regulations[11] require employers and self-employed persons to maintain, so far as is reasonably practicable, electrical systems and electrical equipment within their control. Electrical equipment will include appliances such as washing machines, vacuum cleaners, irons, food preparation machinery etc.

162 Electricity can cause shock, burns and start fires. It should therefore never be treated lightly. Electrical equipment within work premises should be installed and maintained by a competent person. If using an outside contractor, one way of demonstrating competence would be to select an organisation who is certificate holder of the National Inspection Council for Electrical Installation Contracting (NICEIC).

Fixed electrical installations

163 All fixed electrical installations should be designed, installed, operated and maintained to prevent electrical danger. The Institution of Electrical Engineers produces guidance on testing and inspection of fixed installations. This is now in its sixteenth edition and is called the 'Regulations for Electrical Installations'. This is recognised as a British Standard (BS 7671: 1992). It should be remembered that despite its title, these are *not* a legal requirement.

164 The Institution of Electrical Engineers recommend that fixed electrical installations should be inspected and tested at regular intervals, and for residential care homes this would normally be done at least once every three years. This should be done by a competent person who should advise of any defects and prepare a report indicating such defects. All defects considered serious by the competent person should be remedied as soon as possible after being reported. The possession of such a report and a suitable defect remedy system is one way of demonstrating compliance with the Electricity at Work Regulations 1989, in respect of maintenance of the installation.

165 Providing sufficient 13 amp socket outlets fitted with switches will avoid the use of multi-adaptors. It is recommended that socket outlets in homes for the elderly or persons with physical disabilities should be approximately one metre above floor level and easily accessible. Switches and socket outlets sited outdoors should be appropriate for that use, ie of weatherproof construction. Only equipment designed for use outdoors should be used in that environment.

Portable equipment

166 Sufficient socket outlets for working areas will reduce the need for trailing cables across floors. Where vacuum cleaners are used, extra care should be taken to ensure the cable from the machine does not pose a tripping hazard, especially to elderly or poor-sighted residents.

167 Damaged cables should generally be replaced completely. Never carry out makeshift repairs to cables. When joining flexible cables, proper connectors should be used, ie not chocolate block connectors.

168 Regular in-house visual checks of equipment should be carried out to ensure cables are in good condition, plugs are correctly attached and the equipment is in general good repair. These can be undertaken by the users before and during use. Staff who have received the necessary training may be able to check the fuse rating or earthing connection of the electrical equipment. However, no-one should carry out electrical work unless they have sufficient knowledge to prevent a danger to themselves or others. Some equipment belonging to residents may also need to be inspected since this can have an impact on the safety of others in the home. There should always be an initial visual check when items are first brought onto the premises. Staff should be encouraged to report any

evident electrical problem, for example, broken plugs, frayed flex, discoloured or overheated cables. Defective or unsuitable equipment should be withdrawn from service until it is either repaired or destroyed.

169 Portable equipment (such as vacuum cleaners and irons used by staff), which is subject to constant and heavy use, may need more than the occasional visual check to ensure that it is safe and will not give rise to danger. There is no requirement under the Regulations for regular testing, although some electrical testing may be necessary. It is clearly sensible to keep records of all the inspections and tests carried out on each piece of equipment. Where portable devices such as residual current devices (RCDs) are in use, they will also need to be adequately maintained.

170 There have been a number of reported accidents relating to burn injuries to the hands/arm caused by sparks from irons. This type of accident probably results from a frayed cable as it enters the iron's body. Visual inspection of such equipment would help to detect this type of fault.

Kitchen safety

171 Kitchens in residential care homes vary from domestic type kitchens in small homes where residents take some part in preparing their own meals to commercially designed kitchens fully equipped to meet the needs of a large home.

Layout

172 The layout of the kitchen will depend upon its area and the items of equipment in it. There should always be enough room around equipment for staff and residents to move around safely without bumping into each other.

173 Persons using knives and other hand tools should have enough room to work safely. There have been incidents when one person has accidently stabbed another because they were working in cramped conditions.

174 There should be enough room to move trolleys and to carry trays and hot food safely. This is particularly important around equipment which has an exposed hot surface, for example, a griddle top. Attention to manual handling techniques is particularly important in kitchens where loads and surfaces may be hot and floors wet.

175 Side hinged doors and bottom hinged doors that open just above floor level should not obstruct a gangway.

176 Hazards can be created by placing some items of equipment next to others, for example, a deep fat fryer next to a sink, or a shelf above an open top cooking range.

Floors

177 Slips are the main cause of accidents in kitchens. A slip-resistant floor surface should be provided in kitchens and serveries. The floor should be kept in a good condition and suitable measures taken to prevent the contamination of floors by liquids. Spillages of any kind should be cleaned immediately.

Equipment

178 All catering equipment should be installed on a level surface on a secure base. For mobile equipment, where castors are fitted the brakes should be regularly checked to make sure they are working properly. Smaller pieces of equipment that sit on a work top should be stable and positioned so that they cannot be dislodged.

179 Some equipment such as food slicers, mincers, food processors etc have dangerous parts and should be fitted with guards to protect the user. Guards should be checked before the equipment is used and maintained in good order. A visual examination should be made and any broken or missing guards should be repaired or replaced. Anyone using such equipment should receive appropriate training.

180 Catering equipment has to be stripped down for cleaning. The equipment should be isolated from the electrical supply before cleaning commences. It should be possible to clean guards easily and thoroughly and they should be replaced after cleaning. Equipment should not be run if any guard has been removed.

Use of pesticides in kitchens

181 If pesticides need to be used in the kitchen, care should be taken to ensure work surfaces and equipment are not contaminated. Where contamination is suspected, they should be cleaned before use. When pesticides are applied by a pest control operator, staff should liaise with such operatives for advice on the products used, whether the treated area can be entered, precautions to be taken etc. The use of pesticides should be considered when making the COSHH assessment.

Laundry safety

Machinery

182 In most residential care homes the washing machines and tumble driers are used extensively and in some homes by residents as well as staff.

183 The machine suppliers or manufacturers should give you information which should be followed with regards to maintenance, electrical safety, prevention of fire hazards, cleaning of equipment and turning off water and electrical supplies to the machines in the event of an emergency. Maintenance should be carried out by a competent person.

184 The movement of machinery parts can pose a hazard to staff and residents, therefore machines should be fitted with an interlock mechanism which prevents the machine from being set in motion until the front-loading door is closed and which keeps it closed until any dangerous moving parts have come to rest. It is acceptable for top-loading machines to be opened during agitation but the machine should be fitted with devices which prevent the transition from agitation to spin until the lid is closed and which keeps it closed until any dangerous moving parts have come to rest.

185 With tumble and spin driers it is equally important to ensure that opening the door cuts off the electrical supply bringing the cylinder to a halt. The electrical interlock switch used for this purpose should also prevent powered rotation of the cylinder until the door is closed.

186 A member of staff should be designated to carry out periodic checks on the interlocking devices on the machines. This can be done simply by trying to start the machines with the doors open and also attempting to open the doors while the machines are running. A reporting system could be set up so that any user noticing that the machine continues to run after the door has been opened or has any other defect, passes this information to the person in control.

Handling soiled laundry

187 Procedures should be laid down for the handling of soiled laundry. Soiled laundry should be kept separate from other dirty laundry and should be identified as such, so that suitable precautions can be taken by the laundry staff. A COSHH assessment similar to that for clinical waste should be carried out for soiled laundry.

188 Heavily soiled laundry should be sluiced in a specially designated sluice sink or sluice machine and never in a bath or sink used for hand washing clothes. Where there is incontinence or likelihood of incontinence, a washing machine with a foul linen wash may be used. Soiled laundry subjected to a hot wash programme of 65 degrees for 10 minutes or 71 degrees for 3 minutes, will reduce any subsequent contamination risk.

189 A wash hand basin together with a hot and cold water supply, bacteriocidal soap and disposable paper towels sited in the sluice room, will ensure that any contamination that has taken place is easily and quickly removed without the risk of spreading to other areas.

Outdoor health and safety

190 The safety of staff, residents and visitors will extend to garden and outdoor areas. Steps and paths should be kept in good condition and free from obstructions which could lead to tripping hazards, eg refuse and gardening equipment. In winter, gritting and salting steps and paths in anticipation of frost and ice will help to prevent slipping. It may be necessary at times to create a safe pathway through snow. Steps should have a suitable handrail and paths which are used in the hours of darkness should be provided with outdoor lighting. A simple check may be necessary to establish whether a garden pond is a substantial risk to residents (and also visitors). If appropriate, then some protection against falling in may be needed.

191 Sensible, protective footwear should be worn when mowing the lawn. It is safer to mow across sloping areas, rather than up and down. When using electric mowers, the cable should be kept out of the way of the mower blade and inspected frequently or prior to use. All plugs, sockets and connectors used in any electric mower cables should be suitable for outdoor use; domestic 13 amp plugs and sockets are not suitable for use in wet or dirty conditions. BS 1363 fittings are suitable when marked with IP43 or IP44. Where there is a harmonised European standard this would also be appropriate. The electrical supply to any hand held or hand manipulated electrical equipment used outdoors should be controlled by a

Residual Current Device (RCD). RCDs will offer some protection in the event of a supply cable being severed. Fixed devices should comply with BS 4293: 1983. Portable devices should comply with BS 7071: 1989. Where there is harmonised European standard this would also be appropriate. The test button on the RCD should be operated on a regular basis to ensure the continued effective operation of the device. This is because the devices can develop faults which are not visually apparent.

192 Petrol mower tanks should be filled outdoors and not in a confined space such as a shed or garage. Petrol should only be kept in containers which are designed for that purpose. In the case of unclogging or adjusting the blades, these should always be isolated. This can be achieved by unplugging the electric mower or disconnecting the spark plug on a petrol mower.

193 The Control of Pesticides Regulations 1986 covers the storage and use of all pesticides, for example, fungicides, herbicides, insecticides, public hygiene pest control products, rodenticides and wood preservatives[12].

194 All persons using pesticides should be competent and should have received adequate information and training to use pesticides safely and legally. If pesticides approved for agricultural use are used the operator may require a Certificate of Competence.

195 Only approved pesticides should be used. The instructions on the label should be rigidly adhered to. Where labels have faded and are unreadable, the pesticide should be disposed of safely. Local waste regulation authorities can give advice on disposal, including details of facilities available locally. The waste regulation authorities are:

(a) in England, county councils (for non-metropolitan areas) and district councils or single purpose waste authorities (for metropolitan areas);

(b) in Wales, district councils;

(c) in Scotland, district or island councils.

196 All pesticides should be stored in a suitably constructed, secure bin, cabinet, chest, or vault capable of resisting fire for at least 30 minutes and robust enough to withstand reasonably foreseeable accidental impact. The store needs to be fitted with a sump which will retain the total capacity of the contents stored, in the event of all containers failing simultaneously. It should not be sited within a staff room, office, or any area used for storing or preparing food and if kept outside then it needs to be waterproof. The pesticide store should be identified by a cautionary warning sign (see Figure 2) and smoking

Figure 2

prohibited in the vicinity. For large quantities of pesticides, containers specifically manufactured to comply with legislative requirements for storage, are available on the market. Otherwise, a purpose built pesticide store should be constructed.

Violence to staff

197 Employers are beginning to recognise that violence to staff can be a source of injury and distress. Establishing means to try and reduce aggressive behaviour to employees by residents or their relatives and friends should be considered where the problem exists, rather than accepting violence as an unavoidable occupational hazard. The best way to tackle violence is for employers and employees to work together to decide what to do:

1   Find out if there is a problem.

2   Record all incidents.

3   Classify all incidents.

4   Search for preventive measures.

5   Decide what to do.

6   Put measures into practice.

7   Check that measures work.

198 A flow of information about potentially violent situations within the organisation will help staff to assess the likelihood of violent assault or aggression occurring. This is particularly appropriate when: new members of staff are involved; new residents are admitted; there has been a change in the residents' mental or physical state, medication, behaviour, mood etc; and known violent residents are being transferred to the home. Information on each of these points helps staff to recognise signs of impending disturbance.

199 Each workplace should have a proper system for recording and reporting accidents, incidents and ill-health.

Consideration should be given to including any violent incident by a resident or visitor, whether or not it has led to damage or injury. This may identify critical incidents which may lead to an outbreak of challenging behaviour.

200 The search for preventive measures will generate a range of possibilities. This means that there will often be a number of alternative solutions to a particular problem of violence. However, not all measures will be equally suitable and some will be easier to implement than others. The next step is to decide what measures will be appropriate for the particular situation.

201 There are a number of preventative measures which can be undertaken in the residential care home to prevent and control violence to staff. These include:

(a)   providing equipment such as panic buttons to alert staff to the need for urgent assistance;

(b)   ensuring that staff levels are appropriate to the task, and if there is a high risk whether the level is adequate;

(c)   rotating high risk jobs, ie so that the same person is not always at risk, or doubling up for a particularly unsafe task;

(d)   ensuring that experienced or less vulnerable staff are used for difficult tasks;

(e)   providing adequate, appropriate and proficient information for particular tasks on how to undertake them safely.

202 Training in the prevention and management of violence should be available to all employees who come into contact with residents. In particular, the issue of how to deal with violent incidents should be considered in the basic, post-basic and refresher training of employees. Confidence and capability are important when dealing with a potentially violent incident.

203 General social skills help put people at ease. Establishing a relationship of trust and understanding with the resident, will help to ensure that tensions and anxieties are expressed before they reach a stage where they are released through violent behaviour. A combination of experience in dealing with such problems, personality and training are likely to be the crucial determinants in lessening the risk of violence.

204 It is important to have a plan, drawn up jointly between management and staff, for dealing with violent attacks when they occur. The plan should, where possible, involve residents so that they are aware of the effects of their behaviour, and options which are open to them and the staff for coping with this issue. The following points should be considered:

(a) what action individual members of staff are expected to take;

(b) clear guidance on reporting procedures (both physical recording of incident details and notification to others);

(c) all employees to be aware that such a plan exists and their role within it.

205 Monitoring and reviewing the effect of the measures will allow for effective measures to be identified and sustained, ensuring that resources are directed at those areas which need it most. It also enables less effective measures to be identified and replaced or modified.

206 After a violent incident has occurred, apart from providing assistance for the victim, a number of important personnel and procedural matters should be implemented (see paragraph 204). Following normal operating procedures as soon as is reasonably practicable, will ensure that other residents are not unduly alarmed or disturbed.

207 Management and employees (and in some cases residents) often find it helpful to hold a case meeting following a violent incident to discuss the events leading up to the violence, the behaviour of the resident and the consequences of the resident's actions. A successful discussion may highlight the reason for the incident and enable the staff to defuse such a situation, should it reoccur, to prevent future violence. For example, a pattern may emerge showing that a resident may dislike a particular member of staff or visitor.

Advice on safety policy statements

1   Written safety policy statements are only required if there are five or more employees. The statement may be considered as being in three parts:

  (a)   the statement of the employer's general policy with regard to the health and safety of their employees;

  (b)   the organisation for carrying out the policy; and

  (c)   the arrangements for carrying out the policy.

2   The statement should cover the intent to comply with current statutory provisions and should lay particular emphasis on safe work routines. It should stress the importance of co-operation from the workforce and of good communications at all levels in the business. The statement should be signed by the employer or a partner or senior director.

3   Where necessary the statement should clearly define the responsibilities of named senior and junior members of staff with regard to health and safety generally, and to emergency situations. Those named must have adequate information and authority to perform their responsibilities.

4   It is important that any likely hazards and the extent of health and safety matters under the employer's control are identified. Hazards can be listed together with the rules and precautions for avoiding them and arrangements for dealing with injury, fire and other emergencies should be made clear. The arrangements for providing instruction, training and supervision should also be identified.

5   The general policy should be monitored and kept under review and the statement amended where necessary. The original statement and any subsequent revision must be brought to the notice of all employees. Newly recruited employees should not be overlooked.

6   Employers should write policy statements according to their own needs. It must be emphasised that the written word does not prevent accidents and it is the thorough implementation and application of an effective policy that can play an important part in accident prevention.

7   The priced HSE booklet *Writing your health and safety policy statement*[13] is recommended. It gives guidance on the preparation of a statement, laying out the important points using page by page examples.

Training check list

1   The following check list shows what may need to be considered when preparing a typical training programme.

Decide what training is required and who needs it

2   Will training be 'on' or 'off' the job?

Who will carry out the training?

Who will supervise the training?

What records will be kept?

Decide what the objectives are

3   How is the trainee to be selected? Selection should take account of the physical and mental demands of the job.

How much does the trainee know already about safe working practices?

Choose the method of training

4   For each task prepare a list of all the points training should cover, eg:

what equipment or substance to use;

how the equipment or substance works and what it does;

what dangers are associated with its use, including accidental spillage;

what safety precautions are needed and how they protect the user;

how to clean equipment safely;

what to do if equipment seems faulty;

what personal protective equipment to wear.

Carry out the training

5   Set the trainee to work under close supervision.

Make sure the supervisor has the time and knowledge to supervise effectively.

Make sure the supervisor watches to see that dangerous practices do not develop.

Check the training has worked

6   Check that the trainee knows how to carry out the work properly and safely. Make sure they can be left to work safely without close supervision and monitor performance on a regular basis. (It should be noted that as relationships strengthen between staff and residents, the staff may be encouraged to undertake unsafe tasks by residents requiring a favour.)

Your questions answered

Do I have to provide staff with a staff room?

In the case of new workplaces in operation from 1 January 1993, a separate rest room should be provided. For existing workplaces a rest area is sufficient. Rest areas or rest rooms should be large enough and have sufficient chairs and tables, for the number of employees likely to use them at any one time. Arrangements should be made to protect non-smokers from discomfort caused by tobacco smoke.

Do I have to provide separate staff toilets?

Generally staff should have separate toilet facilities to those provided for residents. However, in small homes where space is at a premium this may not be practicable. Where facilities are shared the number of sanitary conveniences and washing facilities should be increased if necessary. Some Environmental Health Departments may insist on separate toilet facilities for kitchen staff for food hygiene reasons.

What is the poster I have to display?

The Health and Safety Information for Employees Regulations 1989 requires that the poster 'Health and Safety Law - what you should know' is displayed in a location where employees have access. The address of the enforcing authority (ie the local environmental health department or HSE office) and the Employment Medical Advisory Service (EMAS) should be completed at the appropriate place on the poster. Alternatively a leaflet with the same title may be handed to each employee. The poster can be purchased from HSE Books (see back cover).

Some of my staff go home wearing their work overalls, is this a good idea?

Staff should, where possible, change into and out of their work overalls at work. This helps to prevent any infection being taken home by the staff and just as importantly prevents infections being brought into the care home.

What is a competent person?

Generally, this will mean a person with enough practical and theoretical knowledge and actual experience to carry out a particular task safely and effectively, without putting themself or others at risk. They should have the necessary ability in the particular operation of the type of plant and equipment with which they are concerned, an understanding of relevant statutory requirements and an appreciation of the hazards involved. Therefore a qualified electrician who is a competent person in respect of checking the wiring of the premises would not necessarily be a competent person for repairing the passenger lift. In certain circumstances, it is possible to appoint appropriate organisations (eg insurance companies or inspection bodies) to carry out tasks designated for competent persons. The term may have a more restricted meaning in respect of particular regulations.

Can persons other than the employer report accidents to the enforcing authority?

Your safety policy should lay down procedures to be followed in the event of a reportable injury, disease or dangerous occurrence. In the employer's absence there should be provision for a designated person to be given responsibility for reporting accidents.

Can I change an electric plug or do I need to employ an electrician?

Providing you have the necessary basic knowledge to undertake this task without putting yourself or others at risk, there is nothing to stop you tackling this type of work.

Self audit check list

The following check list may be used to help direct your attention to areas in the care home which require regular examination. It is by no means an exhaustive list and should be adapted to suit your particular home.

1   Records

Are they up to date, eg lifts; equipment; boiler; accident/incident; staff training?

Is there an accident book? Do staff know where it is?

Are all reportable accidents reported to the enforcing authority?

Are all assessments (eg general, COSHH, manual handling, personal protective equipment) up-to-date? Are the results implemented in working procedures/practices?

2   Procedures

Do they need updating? Is a review of safety policy and management policies required?

Arrangements for liaising with contractors, employment agencies, etc

Procedures for consulting with staff and union safety representatives

3   Staff training

Are all staff trained (including night staff)?

Is training adequate and suitable?

Is refresher training provided?

Are all agency staff/contractors informed of policies and procedures?

Is sufficient supervision provided?

How is the effectiveness of the training evaluated?

4   First aid

Is the first-aid box fully stocked?

Is staff training up-to-date?

5   COSHH (Chemicals)

Are the health hazards from all substances assessed?

Are control measures implemented?

Are staff trained about safe procedures, use of protective clothing?

Are procedures for spillages in place?

Are new staff *trained* before using substances?

6 COSHH (blood-borne diseases)

Have assessments been made?

Are staff trained in safe working procedures?

Are safe procedures implemented and followed?

Are staff given appropriate protective equipment/ clothing and is it used?

Are cuts, grazes etc always covered with waterproof dressings?

Are basic hygiene procedures in place, including regular hand washing?

Are there procedures for cleaning up spillages?

Do staff know what to do in an accident? (encourage bleeding, liberally wash wound with soap and water, report and record accident)

Are staff offered Hepatitis B immunisation?

7 Clinical waste

Is all clinical waste properly bagged in yellow bags?

Is clinical waste segregated from general waste?

Are sharps disposed of in properly constructed sharps containers?

Is the waste storage area safe, secure, clean and tidy?

Is waste regularly collected?

Are there procedures to deal with spillages?

8 Drugs

Are cupboard locked?

Are residents' drugs in locked cupboard in bedroom?

9 Water temperatures

Are thermostatic mixing valves operating at required temperature?

Is the temperature comfortable (not too hot or cold)?

10 Manual handling

Is manual handling avoided where possible, eg by providing lifting aids or altering work methods?

Have all manual handling tasks been assessed for risks and preventive measures implemented?

Do assessments cover the load, work method, workplace, working environment and individual capability?

Are appropriate lifting aids available and used?

Is equipment, eg beds, adjustable where possible?

Are all staff trained in use of equipment and handling techniques as appropriate?

Are there sufficient staff to carry out handling work?

10 Floors

Are there slippy surfaces?

Have spillages been cleaned up?

Are carpets frayed, flat, even?

Are floor surfaces suitable, non-slip, flat, properly maintained?

Are there obstructions, tripping hazards?

12 Stairs

Are they well-lit?

Is the stair covering in good condition and clean ?

Are there obstructions?

13 Lighting

Are all bulbs working?

Are lighting levels sufficient?

Are lighting levels sufficient including corridors and stairs?

14 Ventilation

Is the atmosphere 'fresh'?

Are there odours?

Are there draughts?

If there sufficient fresh air?

Have chemicals, fumes, steam/condensation been removed?

15 Windows

Are restraints in place?

Is glazing in good condition?

16 Electrical safety

Is it suitable and safe?

Are appliances in good condition?

Are plugs, sockets, leads in good condition?

Are there trailing leads?

Are appliances correctly fused?

Are there enough sockets (ie sockets not overloaded)?

Are circuit breakers used, eg for lawn mowers?

Are regular checks carried out?

Is equipment taken out of use if faulty and promptly repaired?

Do only competent people check and maintain equipment?

Are staff trained in safe use of equipment?

17 Protective equipment

Is protective equipment (eg gloves, aprons, overalls, goggles) suitable, safe, comfortable?

Is it appropriate, properly stored, cleaned and maintained?

Are staff trained how to use it?

18 Kitchen safety

Are machines properly guarded?

Are floors clean?

Is there room to move around safely?

Is ventilation sufficient?

Are staff trained in kitchen hygiene, use of equipment etc?

Is food stored correctly, at correct temperatures etc?

Are floors clean, slip-resistant and dry?

19 Violence

Is there a reporting system in place?

Do staff know how to and encouraged to report incidents?

Is an assessment of risks of violence made and problems identified?

Have a range of preventative measures been considered (eg environment, staffing, personal security, training)?

Are preventative measures implemented?

Are effectiveness of measures monitored?

20 Welfare

Are there adequate toilet and washing facilities?

Are facilities clean and well-maintained?

Is storage provided for staff belongings?

Are staff provided with sufficient restbreaks?

Are smoke-free areas provided?

Is the home regularly cleaned, in good repair and decorative order?

21 Laundry

Are machine interlocks working?

Is there separation of soiled laundry ?

22 Outside

Are paths and steps in good condition and well-lit at night?

Are pesticides locked away?

Example form F2508 for reporting injuries and dangerous occurrences

HSE
Health & Safety
Executive

Health and Safety at Work etc Act 1974
Reporting of Injuries, Diseases and Dangerous Occurrences Regulations 1985

Spaces below
are for office
use only

Report of an injury or dangerous occurrence

- Full notes to help you complete this form are attached.
- This form is to be used to make a report to the enforcing authority under the requirements of Regulations 3 or 6.
- Completing and signing this form does not constitute an admission of liability of any kind, either by the person making the report or any other person.
- If more than one person was injured as a result of an accident, please complete a separate form for each person.

A   Subject of report *(tick appropriate box or boxes)* — *see note 2*

Fatality ☐	Specified major injury or condition ☐	"Over three day" injury ☐	Dangerous occurrence ☐	Flammable gas incident (fatality or major injury or condition) ☐	Dangerous gas fitting ☐
	1	2	3	4	5	6

B   Person or organisation making report (ie person obliged to report under the Regulations) — *see note 3*

Name and address —

Post code —

Name and telephone no. of person to contact —

Nature of trade, business or undertaking —

If in construction industry, state the total number of your employees —

and indicate the role of your company on site *(tick box)* —

Main site contractor ☐ 7   Sub contractor ☐ 8   Other ☐ 9

If in farming, are you reporting an injury to a member of your family? *(tick box)*   ☐ Yes   ☐ No

C   Date, time and place of accident, dangerous occurrence or flammable gas incident — *see note 4*

Date ☐☐ 19 ☐   *day month year*   Time —

Give the name and address if different from above —

Where on the premises or site —
and
Normal activity carried on there

ENV

Complete the following sections D, E, F & H if you have ticked boxes, 1, 2, 3 or 5 in Section A. Otherwise go straight to Sections G and H.

D The injured person — *see note 5*

Full name and address —

Age ☐   Sex ☐ (M or F)   Status *(tick box)* —   Employee ☐ 10   Self employed ☐ 11   Trainee (YTS) ☐ 12

Trainee (other) ☐ 13   Any other person ☐ 14

Trade, occupation or job title —

Nature of injury or condition and the part of the body affected —

F2508 (04/92)

continued overleaf

E Kind of accident - *see note 6*

Indicate what kind of accident led to the injury or condition (*tick one box*) —

Contact with moving machinery or material being machined ☐ 1	Injured whilst handling lifting or carrying ☐ 5	Trapped by something collapsing or overturning ☐ 8	Exposure to an explosion ☐ 12	
Struck by moving, including flying or falling, object. ☐ 2	Slip, trip or fall on same level ☐ 6	Drowning or asphyxiation ☐ 9	Contact with electricity or an electrical discharge ☐ 13	Spaces below are for office use only.
Struck by moving vehicle ☐ 3	Fall from a height* ☐ 7	Exposure to or contact with a harmful substance ☐ 10	Injured by an animal ☐ 14	
Struck against something fixed or stationary ☐ 4	*Distance through which person fell ☐ (metres)	Exposure to fire ☐ 11	Other kind of accident (give details in Section H) ☐ 15	☐

F Agent(s) involved — *see note 7*

Indicate which, if any, of the categories of agent or factor below were involved (*tick one or more of the boxes*) —

Machinery/equipment for lifting and conveying ☐ 1	Process plant, pipework or bulk storage ☐ 5	Live animal ☐ 9	Ladder or scaffolding ☐ 13
Portable power or hand tools ☐ 2	Any material, substance or product being handled, used or stored. ☐ 6	Moveable container or package of any kind ☐ 10	Construction formwork, shuttering and falsework ☐ 14
Any vehicle or associated equipment/machinery ☐ 3	Gas, vapour, dust, fume or oxygen deficient atmosphere ☐ 7	Floor, ground, stairs or any working surface ☐ 11	Electricity supply cable, wiring, apparatus or equipment ☐ 15
Other machinery ☐ 4	Pathogen or infected material ☐ 8	Building, engineering structure or excavation/underground working ☐ 12	Entertainment or sporting facilities or equipment ☐ 16
			Any other agent ☐ 17

Describe briefly the agents or factors you have indicated —

G Dangerous occurrence or dangerous gas fitting — *see notes 8 and 9*

Reference number of dangerous occurrence ☐   Reference number of dangerous gas fitting ☐

H Account of accident, dangerous occurrence or flammable gas incident - *see note 10*

Describe what happened and how. In the case of an accident state what the injured person was doing at the time —

Signature of person making report ☐   Date ☐

Example form F2508A for reporting cases of diseases

HSE
Health & Safety
Executive

Health and Safety at Work etc Act 1974
Reporting of Injuries Diseases and Dangerous Occurrences Regulations 1985

For HSE use

Report of a case of disease

● This form is to be used to make a report to the enforcing authority under the requirements of Regulation 5.
● Completing and signing this form does not constitute an admission of liability of any kind, either by the person making the report or any other person.

A   **Person or organisation making report**
(ie person obliged to report under the Regulations)

Name and address

Post code

Name of person to contact for further inquiry

Tel. No.

Nature of trade, business or undertaking

B   **Details of the person affected**

Surname

Forenames

Date of birth
day   month   year

Sex (M or F)

Occupation

Please indicate whether Employee
(tick box)

Other person

If not an employee, what is the ill person's status?
(eg self-employed or trainee)

F2508A (1/86)

continued overleaf

C   **Details of the disease which is being reported**
(a full list of diseases which are reportable is given in the accompanying notes)

For HSE Use

Name or schedule number of the disease

Date of doctor's statement which
first diagnosed the disease

		19	
day	*month*		*year*

Doctor's name and address, if known

Post code

D   **Description of work giving rise to this report**

Describe any work of the affected person which might be relevant to the onset
of the disease. If the disease is thought to have been caused by the ill person's
exposure to an agent at work (eg a specific chemical) please state what the suspected
agent is.

ENV

E   **Any other relevant information**

Signature of person making report   Date

Factors/questions when making an assessment of manual handling operations

Schedule 1

Factors to which the employer must have regard and questions he must consider when making an assessment of manual handling operations

Regulation 4(1)(b)(i) of the

Manual Handling Operations Regulations 1992

Column 1	*Column 2*
Factors	*Questions*

1 The task

Does it involve:

- holding load at distance from trunk?

- unsatisfactory bodily movement or posture,

  especially:

  - twisting the trunk?

  - stooping?

  - reaching upwards?

- excessive movement of load, especially:

  - excessive lifting or lowering distances?

  - excessive carrying distances?

- excessive pushing or pulling distances?

- risk of sudden movement of load?

- frequent or prolonged physical effort?

- insufficient rest or recovery periods?

Schedule

2 The load

Is it:

- heavy?

- bulky or unwieldy?

- difficult to grasp?

- unstable, or with contents likely to shift?

- sharp, hot or otherwise potentially damaging?

3 The working environment

Are there:

- space constraints preventing good posture?

- uneven, slippery or unstable floors?

- variations in level of floors or work surfaces?

- extremes of temperature, humidity or air movement?

- poor lighting conditions?

4 Individual capability

Does the job:

- require unusual strength, height, etc?

- create a hazard to those who are pregnant or have a health problem?

- require special knowledge or training for its safe performance?

References

British Standards

BS 6642 Disposable plastics refuse sacks made from polyethylene

BS 7320 Sharps containers

BS 6262 Code of practice for glazing in buildings

BS 5655 Lifts and service lifts

BS 5900 Powered domestic lifts

BS 5776 Powered stairlifts (due to be revised shortly)

BS 7671 Requirements for electrical installations. IEE Wiring Regulations. 16th edition

References

1 Draft Guide to Fire Precautions in Residential Care Premises. Available from the Fire and Emergency Planning Department, Home Office, Queen Anne's Gate, London SW11 9AT

2 L21 *Management of Health and Safety at Work: Management of Health and Safety at Work Regulations 1992:* Approved Code of Practice ISBN 0 7176 0412 8

3 HS(R)23 *Guide to the Reporting of Injuries, Diseases and Dangerous Occurrences Regulations 1985* 1986 ISBN 0 7176 0432 2

4 COP 42 *First Aid at Work: Health and Safety (First Aid) Regulations 1981* 1990 ISBN 0 7176 0426 8

5 IND(G)136(L) *COSHH A brief guide for employers. The requirements of the Control of Substances Hazardous to Health (Regulations) 1988*

6 L8 *The prevention or control of legionellosis (including legionnaires' disease)* 1991 ISBN 0 7176 0457 8

7 HS(G)70 *The control of legionellosis including legionnaires' disease*: Approved Code of Practice 1991 ISBN 0 7176 0451 9

8 L23 *Manual Handling:Manual Handling Operations Regulations 1992. Guidance on Regulations* ISBN 0 7176 0411 X

9 L24 *Workplace Health, Safety and Welfare. Workplace (Health, Safety and Welfare) Regulations 1992:* Approved Code of Practice and guidance ISBN 0 7176 0413 6

10 *Safety of passenger lifts in private nursing/ residential care homes improving the safety of 'homelifts'* 1986

11 HS(R)25 *Memorandum of guidance on the Electricity at Work Regulations 1989* 1989 ISBN 0 7176 0433 5

12 HSE *Writing your health and safety policy statement.* rev ed 1989 ISBN 0 7176 0424 1

Further reading

Asbestos Materials in Buildings Department of Environment ISBN 0 11 752370 4

A step by step guide to COSHH assessment HS(G)97 1993 ISBN 0 7176 0421 7

Control of substances hazardous to health and control of carcinogenic substances. Control of Substances Hazardous to Health Regulations 1988. Approved Code of Practice L5 4th ed 1993 ISBN 0 7176 0427 6

Essentials of health and safety at work (revised) 1994 ISBN 0 7176 0716 X

First aid needs in your workplace: your questions answered IND(G)3(L)(rev) 1990 Free leaflet

Flexible leads, plugs, sockets etc GS 37 1985 ISBN 0 11 883519 X

Getting to grips with manual handling IND(G)143(L) (Free leaflet)

Guidance for Clinical Health Care Workers: Protection against infection with HIV and Hepatitis Viruses Recommendations of the expert advisory group on AIDS Department of Health ISBN 0 11 321249 6

Guidance on manual handling of loads in the health service HSE HSAC 1992 ISBN 0 7176 0430 6

Guide to the Health and Safety at Work etc Act 1974 (revised) L1 1990 ISBN 0 7176 0441 1

Health and Safety at Work etc Act: advice to employees HSC 5 1993 Free leaflet

Health and Safety at Work etc Act: advice to employers HSC 3 1993 Free leaflet

Health and safety in kitchens and food preparation areas HS(G)55 1990 ISBN 0 7176 0492 6

Home Life: A Code of Practice for Residential Care Centre for Policy on Ageing (CPA) 1984

Homes are for living in Department of Health Social Services Inspectorate 1989 ISBN 0 11 3212291

Institution of Electrical Engineers 'Regulations for Electrical Installations' 16th Edition BS 7671:1992 1991 ISBN 0 852965 10 9

It's your job to manage safety IND(G)103(L) 1991 Free leaflet

Legionnaires' disease IAC/L27 1992 Free leaflet

Lighten the load: guidance for employees on musculo-skeletal disorders IND(G)110(L) 1991 Free leaflet

Lighten the load: guidance for employers on musculo-skeletal disorders IND(G)109(L) 1991 Free leaflet

New Health and Safety at Work Regulations IND(G)124(L) 1992 Free leaflet

Passive smoking at work IND(G)63L (revised) 1992 Free leaflet

Preventing violence to staff HSE 1988 ISBN 0 11 885467 4

Radon in the Workplace IND(G)123L 1992 Free leaflet

Safe disposal of clinical waste 1992 ISBN 0 7176 0447 0

"Safe" hot water and surface temperatures NHS Estates Guidance Note: 1992 ISBN 0 11 321404 9

Safe use of portable electrical apparatus (electrical safety) PM 32(rev) 1990 ISBN 0 7176 0448 9

Successful health and safety management HS(G)65 1991 ISBN 0 7176 0425 X

The control of asbestos at work : Control of Asbestos at Work Regulations 1987. Approved Code of Practice (2nd edition) L27 ISBN 0 7176 0450 0

The control of legionellae in health care premises: a Code of Practice Department of Health and Social Security 1989 ISBN 0 11 3212089

Violence to staff Department of Health and Social Security 1988 ISBN 0 11 321158 9

Violence to staff IND(G)69(L) 1989 Free leaflet

Violence to staff in the Health Services HSE HSAC 1987 ISBN 0 11 883917 9

Watch your step: prevention of slipping, tripping and falling accidents at work 1985 ISBN 0 11 883782 6

Work with asbestos insulation, asbestos coating and asbestos insulating board: Control of Asbestos at Work Regulations 1987: Approved Code of Practice (2nd edition) L28 ISBN 0 7176 0460 8

Writing a safety policy statement: advice to employers HSC 6 1987 (revised) Free leaflet

Writing your health and safety policy statement: guide to preparing a safety policy statement for a small business (revised) 1989 ISBN 0 7176 0424 1

Printed and published by the Health and Safety Executive

04/99   C15